Schott New York

Gregory Spears

b.1977

Walden

a song cycle for baritone and piano

Full score

ED 30265

SCHOTT

Mainz · London · Madrid · New York · Paris · Prague · Tokyo · Toronto

Commissioned by DC Vocal Arts for Brian Mulligan and Timothy Long

Composer note

I have long admired Thoreau's prose, both for its ideas as well as its stylistic beauty. For this song cycle, I selected a series of excerpts from Walden divided into four structurally interconnected songs and a final coda. These fragments are arranged to loosely tell the story of Thoreau's departure from and return to society in Concord, MA. Along the way we see Thoreau's progression from anxious social critic, to passionate naturalist, to contemplative mystic. The cycle ends with a coda, setting one of Walden's most cryptic passages concerning "a hound, a bay horse, and a turtle-dove." I began composing with spartan materials: a two-note melody supported by piano textures resembling simple finger exercises. As I continued working, the music became more elaborate through the layering and transforming of these humble ideas. Along the way I was inspired by Thoreau's challenge that we should look for the sublime in the simplest, most common materials.

Performance Notes

1. A "U" placed over a note indicates a cancellation of a metrical accent. These notes/syllables should be unaccented.
2. A note with an X notehead indicates the placement of a strong final consonant.
3. A tenuto mark indicates that a note should be emphasized, but without the sharp attack suggested by an accent.

Duration
ca. 27 minutes

World Premiere
September 16, 2018; Washington, DC
The Kennedy Center
Brian Mulligan, baritone • Timothy Long, piano

All texts taken from Henry David Thoreau's *WALDEN; or, Life in the Woods*

I.

I went to the woods because I wished to live deliberately, to front only the essential facts of life, and see if I could not learn what it had to teach, and not, when I came to die, discover that I had not lived. I did not wish to live what was not life, living is so dear; nor did I wish to practice resignation, unless it was quite necessary. I wanted to live deep and suck out all the marrow of life, to live so sturdily and Spartan-like as to put to rout all that was not life, to cut a broad swath and shave close, to drive life into a corner, and reduce it to its lowest terms, and, if it proved to be mean, why then to get the whole and genuine meanness of it, and publish its meanness to the world; or if it were sublime, to know it by experience, and be able to give a true account of it in my next excursion. For most men, it appears to me, are in a strange uncertainty about it, whether it is of the devil or of God...

...the laboring man has not leisure for a true integrity day by day...

It is a fool's life, as they will find when they get to the end of it, if not before.

I hear an irresistible voice which invites me away from all that.

It is no dream of mine,
To ornament a line;
I cannot come nearer to God and Heaven
Than I live to Walden even.
I am its stony shore,
And the breeze that passes o'er;
In the hollow of my hand
Are its water and its sand,
And its deepest resort
Lies high in my thought.

II.

Sometimes, on Sundays, I heard the bells, the Lincoln, Acton, Bedford, or Concord bell, when the wind was favorable, a faint, sweet, and, as it were, natural melody, worth importing into the wilderness. At a sufficient distance over the woods this sound acquires a certain vibratory hum, as if the pine needles in the horizon were the strings of a harp which it swept. All sound heard at the greatest possible distance produces one and the same effect, a vibration of the universal lyre, just as the intervening atmosphere makes a distant ridge of earth interesting to our eyes by the azure tint it imparts to it.

Simplicity, simplicity, simplicity! I say, let your affairs be as two or three, and not a hundred or a thousand; instead of a million count half a dozen, and keep your accounts on your thumb-nail. In the midst of this chopping sea of civilized life, such are the clouds and storms and quicksands and thousand-and-one items to be allowed for, that a man has to live, if he would not founder and go to the bottom and not make his port at all, by dead reckoning, and he must be a great calculator indeed who succeeds.

III.

Time is but the stream I go a-fishing in. I drink at it; but while I drink I see the sandy bottom and detect how shallow it is. Its thin current slides away, but eternity remains. I would drink deeper; fish in the sky, whose bottom is pebbly with stars.

Sometimes, in a summer morning, having taken my accustomed bath, I sat in my sunny doorway from sunrise till noon, rapt in a revery, amidst the pines and hickories and sumachs, in undisturbed solitude and stillness, while the birds sang around or flitted noiseless through the house, until by the sun falling in at my west window, or the noise of some traveller's wagon on the distant highway, I was reminded of the lapse of time.

IV.

I left the woods for as good a reason as I went there. Perhaps it seemed to me that I had several more lives to live, and could not spare any more time for that one.

I learned this, at least, by my experiment: that if one advances confidently in the direction of his dreams, and endeavors to live the life which he has imagined, he will meet with a success unexpected in common hours.

Every one has heard the story which has gone the rounds of New England, of a strong and beautiful bug which came out of the dry leaf of an old table of apple-tree wood, which had stood in a farmer's kitchen for sixty years, first in Connecticut, and afterward in Massachusetts — from an egg deposited in the living tree many years earlier still, as appeared by counting the annual layers beyond it; which was heard gnawing out for several weeks, hatched perchance by the heat of an urn. Who does not feel his faith in a resurrection and immortality strengthened by hearing of this? Who knows what beautiful and winged life, whose egg has been buried for ages under many concentric layers of woodenness in the dead dry life of society, deposited at first in the alburnum of the green and living tree, which has been gradually converted into the semblance of its well-seasoned tomb — heard perchance gnawing out now for years by the astonished family of man, as they sat round the festive board — may unexpectedly come forth from amidst society's most trivial and handselled furniture, to enjoy its perfect summer life at last!...The light which puts out our eyes is darkness to us. Only that day dawns to which we are awake. There is more day to dawn. The sun is but a morning star.

Humility like darkness reveals the heavenly lights. The shadows of poverty and meanness gather around us, 'and lo! creation widens to our view.'

CODA

I long ago lost a hound, a bay horse, and a turtle-dove, and am still on their trail. Many are the travellers I have spoken concerning them, describing their tracks and what calls they answered to. I have met one or two who had heard the hound, and the tramp of the horse, and even seen the dove disappear behind a cloud, and they seemed as anxious to recover them as if they had lost them themselves.

Baritone and Piano

WALDEN

Henry David Thoreau

I.

Gregory Spears

34
41
48
55
mf
f

p
mf un poco marcato
62
I went to the woods be-cause I
mf
f
mf
68
wished to live de - li - bera - tely, to front on-ly the es - sen - tial facts of
74
life, and see if I could not learn what it had to teach, and not, when I

80
came to die, dis - co - ver that I had not lived.
85
I did not wish to live what was not life,
90
liv - ing is so dear; nor did I wish to prac - tice re - sig -

95
mp mf
na - tion, un-less it was quite ne-ces-sa-ry. I want - ed to
100
live deep and suck out all the mar-row of life, to
105
f
live so stur - di-ly and Spar - tan - like as to put to route all that was not
f

110
life, to cut a broad swath and shave close, to drive life in-to a cor-ner,
115
mf
and re-duce it to its low-est terms, and, if it proved to be mean,
120
ff
why then to get the

125
whole and ge - nu-ine mean-ness of it, and pub - lish its mean-ness to the world;
130
mp
p legato e dolce
p
or if it were sub - blime,
136
un poco marcato
to know it by ex - pe - ri-ence, and be a-ble to give a true ac - count of
3

142
it in my next ex - cur - sion.
148
For most men, it ap - pears to me, are in a strange un - cer-tain-ty
154
a-bout it, wheth-er it is of the de - vil or of

159
pp
p
mf
God... ...the la-bor-ing man has not
mp
mf
mp
165
lei - sure for a true in-te - gri-ty day by
mf
(etc.)
170
day... It is a fool's life

175
as they will find when they get to the end of it, if not be-
180
fore. It is a fool's life. It is a fool's life,
185
a fool's
8va
mf

190
life
as they will find.
(8va)
ff
195
It is a fool's
(8va)
(no crescendo)
199
life.
ff

206
mf
legato
e dolce
I hear an ir-re-sis - ti-ble
mf
212
voice which in-vites me a-way.
217
p
f
I hear an ir-re-sis - ti-ble voice
f

222
mp
which in - vites me a - way from all
227
that.
232
p
p
238

243
p
It is no dream of mine, to or - na ment a line; I
249
mf
can - not come near - er to God and Hea - ven than I
mf
molto rallentando
♩ = 134
256
live to Wal - den ev - en.

p
mf
263
I am its sto - ny shore,
270
and the breeze that pas - ses o'er; In the ho - low of my hand Are
277
its wa - ter and its sand, and its deep-est re - sort lies high

285
lies high in my thought.
293
lunga

II.

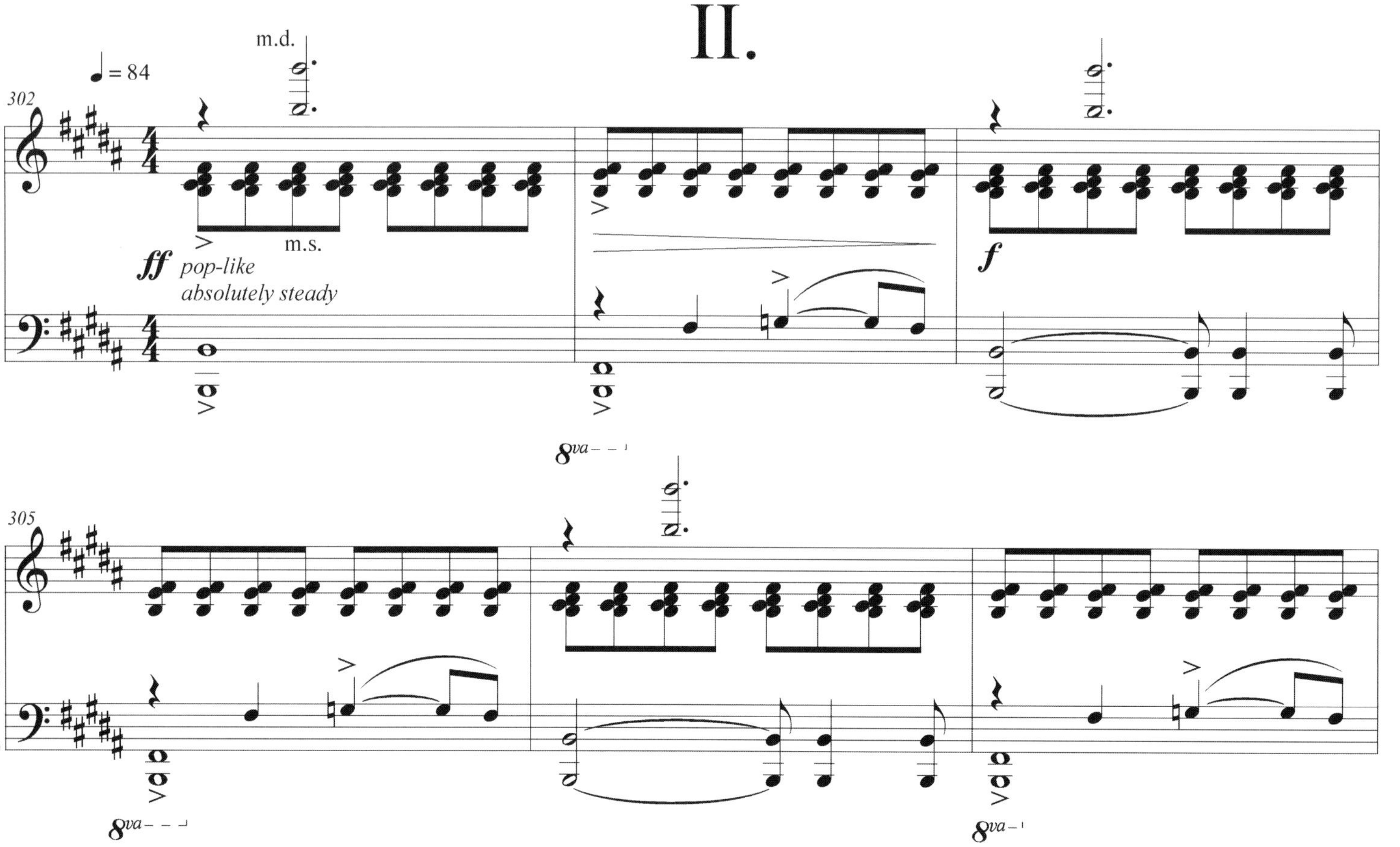
♩ = 84
m.d.
302
ff pop-like
absolutely steady
m.s.
f
8va
305
8va
8va

legato e dolce
playful and buoyant throughout
mf
Some-times, on
Sun - days, I heard the bells,
the Lin-coln, Ac-ton, Bed-ford, or Con-cord bell, when the wind was fa-vo-ra-ble,

317
mp
a faint, sweet, and as it were, na-tur-al me-lo - dy worth im - port-ing in-to the wild-er-ness
mp
8va
321
p
mf
p
At a suf - fi - cient dis - tance o-ver the woods this sound ac-
ff
mf
8va
324
mf
legato
dolce
quires a cer - tain vi-bra-to-ry hum, as if the pine need-les in the ho-
8va

328
ri-zon were the strings of a harp which it swept.
8va
332
All sound heard at the great-est pos-si-ble dis - tance pro-du - des one and the
mp
8va
335
same ef - fect, a vi - bra - tion of the u - ni -
mf
8va

338
ver - sal lyre, just as the in - ter - ven - ing at - mo -
341
phere makes a dis - tant ridge of earth in - terest - ing to our eyes by the a - zure
344
tint it im - parts to it. Sim -

348
pli - ci-ty,
sim - pli - ci-ty,
mf
8va
351
sim - pi - ci - ty! I say, let your af - fairs be as two or three, and not a
mf
355
hun-dred or a thou - sand in stead of a mil-ion count half a do-zen, and
mf

358
keep your ac-counts up-on your thumb - nail. In the midst of this chop-ping sea of
362
ci - vil-ized life, such are the clouds and storms and quick-sands and thou-sand-and-
365
one i - tems to be al - lowed for, that a man has to live if he would
f

369
ff
not found-er and go to the bot-tom and not make his port at all, by dead
f
ff
374
mp
reck - - - on - ing.
p un poco marcato
379
8va

383
p espress. e dolce
and he must be a great cal - cu-la-tor in-deed who suc-ceeds.
388
a great cal-cu-la-tor in-deed who suc - ceeds.
394
pp
401
♩ = 138
mp crisp, strict pulse, quasi-mechanical
Ped.

III.

436
442
f
446
451

455
p
Time is but the stream I go a -
p
460
fish - ing in. I drink at it; but while I drink I see
466
the san - dy bot - tom and de - tect how shal - low it is.

471
Its thin
474
cur - rent, its thin cur - rent slides
478
a-way but e - ter - ni-ty, e -

483
ter - ni-ty
re - mains.
p
487
491
ff
I
would
drink
ff
496
deep - - - - er;
I would drink deep -

500
er; fish in the sky, whose bot-tom is peb-bly with stars.
505
poco meno mosso
p
mf
Some-times, in a sum-mer morn-ing, hav-ing tak-en my ac - cus-tomed bath,
510
I sat in my sun-ny door - way from sun - rise till noon, rapt
516
in a re-ve-ry, a-midst the pines and hick - o - ries and su - machs, in

522
un - dis-turbed so - li-tude and still - ness, while the birds sang a-
528
dolce
round or flit-ted noise - less through the house, un-til by the sun fal - ling
534
in at my west win - dow, or the noise of some tra - vel-ler's wa -
540
gon on the dis-tant high - way, I was re-mind - ed of the lapse

546
the lapse of
552
molto rallentando
♩ = 126
accel.
♩ = 148
time.
558
The lapse of time.
564

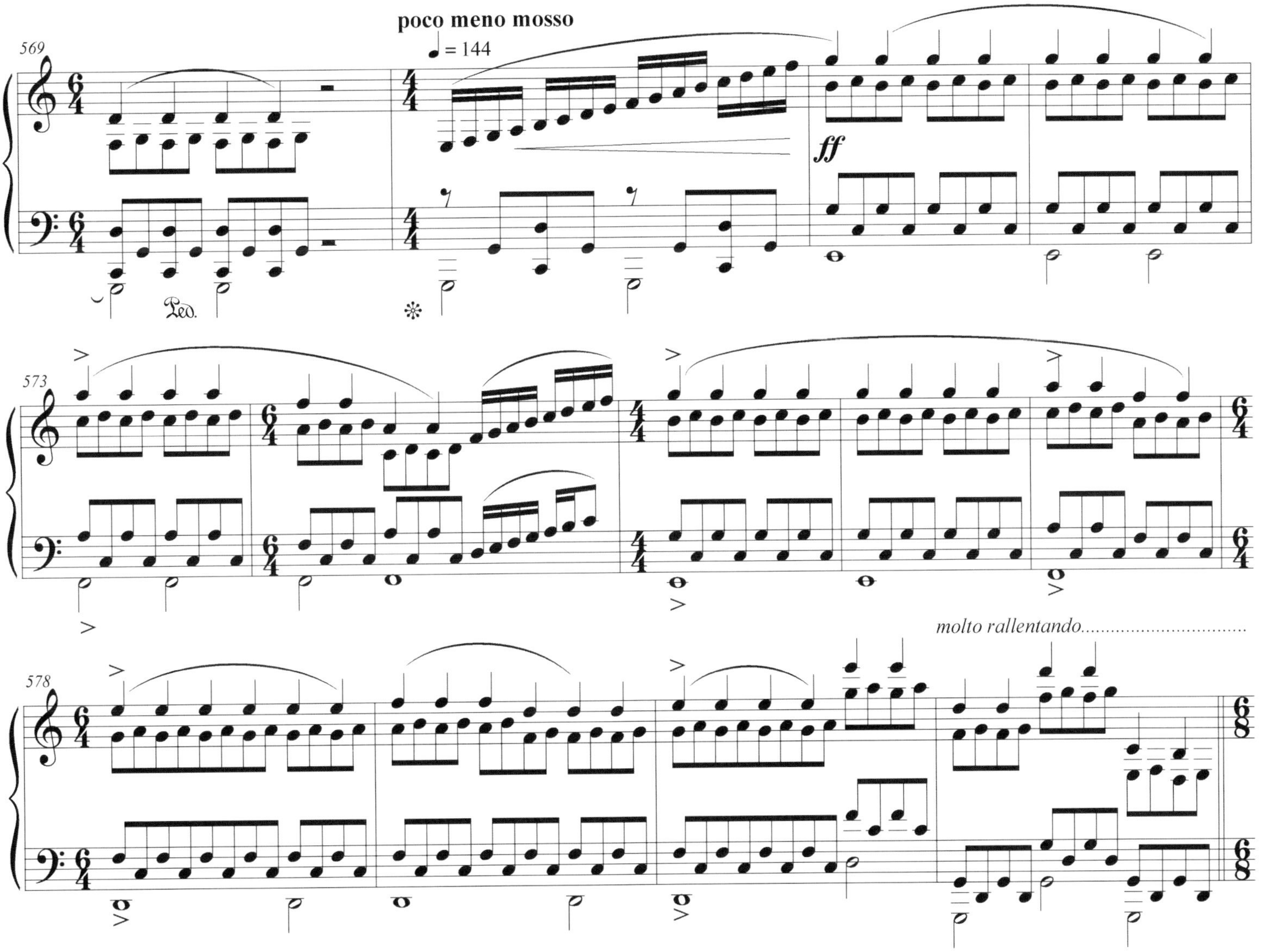
poco meno mosso
♩ = 144
ff
molto rallentando.................................

IV.

♪ = 146
ff crisp, strict pulse, quasi-mechanical
(etc.)
mp

591
mp molto legato
I left the woods for as good a rea - son as I went there.
(etc.)
594
Per-haps it seemed to me that I had se-ve-ral more lives to live, and
598
could not spare an-y more time for that one. I learned this, at least, by my ex-

602
pe - ri-ment: that if one ad-van-ces con - fi-dent - ly in the di-
606
rec - tion of his dreams, and en-dea-vors to live the life which he has i-ma - gined,
609
he will meet with a suc-cess un-ex - pec-ted in com - mon hours.
613
mf
Ped.

617
(etc.)
621
Ev -
625
- - ery one has heard the sto - ry which has gone the rounds of New En -
628
gland, of a strong and beau-ti-ful bug which came out of the

632
dry leaf of an old ta-ble of ap - ple tree
8va
636
wood,
640
which had stood in a far-mer's kit-chen for six - ty years,

643
first in Con-nec-ti-cut, and af - ter-ward in Mas - se-chu - setts,
from an
647
egg de-po-sit-ed in the liv-ing tree ma-ny years ear-li-er still, as ap-peared by count-ing the
650
an-nu-al la-yers be-yond it; which was heard gnaw - ing out for se-ve-ral weeks,
p
p

653
— hatched per - chance by the heat of an urn.
657
661
665

669
p
Who does not feel his faith
673
in a re - sur-rec-tion and im-mor-tal - i-ty streng-thened by hear-ing this?
677
Who knows what beau-ti-ful and wing-ed life, whose egg has been bu-ried for ag - es

681
3
2
un-der ma-ny con-cen-tric lay-ers of wood - en - ness
685
in the dead dry life of so-ci - e - ty, de -
689
pos - i - ted at first in the al - bur - num of the green and liv-ing tree,

692
f
which has been gra-du-al-ly con-vert - ed in-to the sem - blance of its well-sea-soned
f
8va
696
tomb heard per-chance gnaw-ing out now for years by the a-ston-ished fam - i-ly
mf
700
mf
of man, as they sat round the fes - tive board, may un - ex -

704
pec-ted-ly come forth from a-midst so-ci - e-ty's most tri-vi-al and
(loco)
8va
708
hand - selled fur - ni-ture, to en - joy its per - fect sum-mer life at
mf
712
last! To en - joy its
(loco)
8va

715
ff
per - fect sum-mer life at last! The light which
ff subito
(propulsive downbeats)
719
puts out our eyes is dark-ness to us. On - ly that day dawns to which we are a -
722
wake. There is more day to dawn. The sun is but a morn-ing star.

726
Hu - mi - li-ty like dark - ness re - veals the
730
hea - ven - ly lights. The sha-dows of po ver ty and mean - ness gath-er a - round
733
mf
us, 'and lo! cre -

a - tion wid - ens to our view.' Cre -
a - tion wid - ens to our view.
Hu - mi - li-ty like dark - ness re - veals the

hea - ven-ly lights. The sha-dows of po - ver-ty and mean-ness gath-er a - round us, 'and lo!
cre -
a - tion wid - ens to our
attacca

CODA

788
mp
795
802
mp legato
I long a-go lost a hound,
mp
809
a bay - horse,

816
and a tur - tle - dove,
and
823
am still on their trail.
Ma - ny are
830
parlando
the tra - vel - lers
I have spo-ken con - cern-ing them,

836
des-crib-ing their tracks and what calls they ___ an - swer to. ___
842
I have met one or two who had heard the
848
p
hound, ___ and the tramp of the horse, and ev-en seen the
p

855
dove di - sap - pear be - hind a cloud,
862
and they seemed as an-xious to re - co - ver them as
869
if they had lost them them - selves.

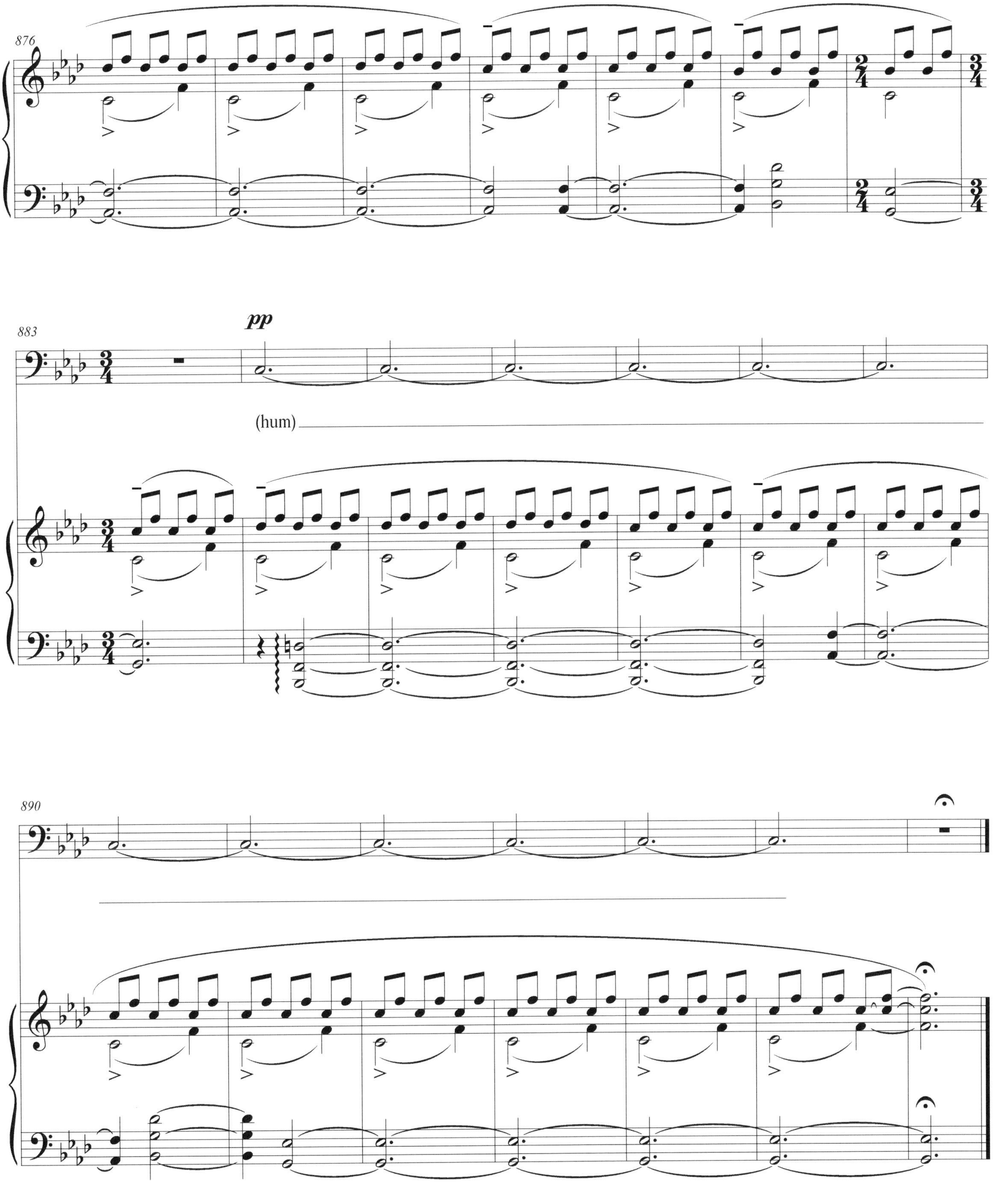
876
883
pp
(hum)
890